Mornings You Might Wake Up In

Near-Essays and Almost-Poems

Hayley G. Hoover

Mornings You Might Wake Up In
Copyright © 2025 Hayley G. Hoover
All rights reserved. This book, or parts thereof, may not be reproduced in any form without permission.

ISBN: 978-1-7351093-1-2 (Paperback)

Edited by Carina Belles
Cover art by Olga Gryb, grybdesigns.com
Cover design by Jordan Edwards, Jordan Edwards Designs

Fuzzball Publishing
First printing edition 2025

For all things hazy, rosy,
candy-colored, and serene

> "So moments pass as though
> they wished to stay.
> We have not long to love.
> A night. A day...."
>
> —Tennessee Williams,
> "We Have Not Long to Love"

Contents

Introduction   13

Part 1: Going Out

Cotton Shirt Little Skirt	19
Valencia	21
Some Types Of People I Like	23
Lawn Chairs Under The Stars	24
Santa Monica Boulevard	26
Cinnamon Nutmeg Allspice Ginger Cloves	28
Jeopardy! Tournament of Champions	29
Chocolate Lava Cakes	31
World Market	33
All Of The Tens	35
Dandelion Sunburst	37
A City I've Never Been To Before	39
Lemon Drop	41
Pet Human	43
Backseat Of An Uber	44
Oath Of Cringe	46

Part 2: Going In

Show Dog	51
Everything You've Ever Wanted	52
Roadmap	54
Brunch Debriefing	56
Easter Sunday	58
Be 22	60
Home Library	62
24-Hour Diner	64
Overcast	66
Favorite Raindrop	68
Sexy Achilles Tendons	70
Ice Skating Rink	71
Okay, One More	73
Screening	75
Cast Iron Tub	76
Art Museum	78

Part 3: In And Out

Touch Grass	83
I Know What I'm Working With	84
Text Post	86
Twilight	87
This Might Be Weird	89
Aristocats	90

Who's Bored Of The Moon?!	92
For You Page	93
It's Probably Fine	95
Boomers	97
Gen X	98
Millennials	99
Gen Z	100
Writer's Block	101
In Pursuit Of Beauty	103
For All You Know	105

Part 4: Falling Out

Spare A Thought For Thigh Gaps	109
Walk-In Closet	111
Tangerine	113
Dopamine Factory	115
Grief Has Felt Like	117
A State Of Kale Smoothie	119
Others	120
Vroom Vroom Grrrr	122
Time Travel	124
Ankle Weights	126
Scrolling	128
Bubbles	130
Reasons I'm Glad To Be Alive In This Century	132

I Do Not Want To Camp	134
Heaven's Pink	136
It Is That You Are	138

Part 5: Falling In

What Do Women Want?	143
It's Entirely Possible	145
Pride And Prejudice	147
Sweat And Glitter	149
Asymmetrical Ceramics	151
Daydreams	153
Sizzling Skillet	155
The Tomatoes	157
Hillside Home	158
The Field Across The Street From The Church	160
Picnic Basket	162
Beach Day	164
The Most Intimate Of Intimacies	166
Mornings You Might Wake Up In	168
Quiet Forest	170
Muscle Memory	172

Mornings You Might Wake Up In

Introduction

We're meeting here in this ink and paper book, but the pieces you're about to read began as social media videos. I wrote them on my phone, almost entirely in the early mornings, while my espresso machine hummed and last night's mascara glued my eyes half shut. What I intended as a collection of little observations and throwaway jokes quickly developed a mind of its own, as so many creative projects do. It grew into what I hope you might find cozy, romantic, sometimes funny and sometimes ruminative, near-essays and almost-poems. You may have seen a few in your feed, though the most vulnerable and intimate among them never got filmed, or never got posted, and are unique to this book. A year's worth of minute-long monologues came together here, as one twisty, breathless soliloquy. I'm calling it *Mornings You Might Wake Up In*, and it has five parts.

The first part is called Going Out, and it's a tribute to the world offline. Going out of your comfort zone, going out on a limb, going out in style, going out dancing in a bar that still smells like cigarette smoke and serves fried dill pickles under those 1980s Victorian-style lampshades that look like stained glass but are actually dusty, hot plastic. It begins with the first piece I wrote in this style, Cotton Shirt Little Skirt, which occupies a special place in my heart for helping me find the voice of this book.

The next section, Going In, is full of shower thoughts and lazy mornings under the crocheted granny square blanket your best friend found at a thrift store in 2010. Going in deep, going in circles, going in blind, going into that introspective place where everything feels poetic and symbolic and you're sure the journal entry you just wrote deserves a Pulitzer even if you won't find it particularly brilliant tomorrow. My favorite piece in the whole book, Roadmap, is tucked into this part.

Part three, In And Out, is the intermission. All the goofy and strange bits. It's named after the way I repeatedly moved them into different parts of this book and then took them out again. And it's named after drive-thru fries covered in onions. Does a book about love and grief and self-reflection need a rant about the cultural impact of the *Twilight* franchise? I ultimately decided it does.

The fourth section is called Falling Out, and it's a mix of anxiety and gratitude. Falling out of step, falling out of touch, falling out of fashion, falling out with yourself over whether you're contributing something positive to the world by making art and sharing it with people, or if you're just feeding your own ego, as well as the voracious AI databases that study your stream of consciousness and use it to build weapons of war that will take us all out in the robot revolution. You'll find the piece that had the biggest impact on my year, Spare A Thought For Thigh Gaps, in here.

Last, we have Falling In, made up of all things dreamy and romantic and confidently cheesy. Falling in place, falling in bed, falling in platonic love with the people who make you feel like you, falling in romantic love with the same person every time they smile at you through the swirl of steam wafting from your teacups. One of my favorites is called What Do Women Want? I feel like it fills the center of the Venn diagram between social media and poetry, and it's my absolute dream that someone out there will feel the same way.

I'm really excited to share these with you. I wonder if you'll find something in here that you like, and I love that I won't get immediate push notifications full of intense comments if you don't. Grab a cup of coffee and a scone. If you find yourself waking up in one of these mornings, I hope you enjoy your stay.

Part 1

Going Out

"Because it's a Wednesday night,
baby, and I'm alive!"

—Hannah Horvath, *Girls*

Cotton Shirt Little Skirt

I don't need a lot to be happy. All I want today is like cotton shirt, little skirt, gold hoops, brown mascara, Glossier You, French baguette, avocado, heirloom tomato, arugula, olive oil, flaky sea salt, cracked black pepper, almond milk latte, big mug, big handle, you know?

Like 75 and sun, Simon and Garfunkel, windows down, farmer's market, fresh basil, red onion, red raspberry, purple garlic, purple peonies, long walk, hold hands, Kacey Musgraves *Golden Hour*, you know?

Like velvet couch contact nap, oxytocin rush, sudden thunderstorm, knit blanket, Anthropologie candle, Gillian Flynn novel, minestrone in a wide-narrow bowl, FaceTime best friend, learn Mitski song on piano, Amaj7 C# D Dm, you know?

Like fold laundry, vacuum, yoga, low-light shower, full-body lotion, hair mask, flannel pajama shorts, lacy tank top, knee-high socks, ice water, glass straw, inside joke, *30*

Rock season four, chana masala, jasmine rice, garlic naan, pinot noir in a crystal glass and trace your finger around the rim, you know?

Like legs in lap, lively debate, *I'm so glad you're the one I'm doing this life with*, play with hair, like *I love you too, you know.*

Valencia

I feel like I would be healed by just one of those 2012 nights when you're doing your makeup, cross-legged on the floor, in front of a full-length, flimsy, five-dollar mirror, listening to Ke$ha on the speakers of a laptop that has a thick, orange plastic cover plastered with stickers that say things like "well behaved women rarely make history," and one of your friends is hanging upside down from the edge of the bed, sharing unnecessary, but appreciated, details about drama at work, and another friend is showing you Tumblr gifs that make it look like *Glee* characters are making out, and another friend is choking you on aerosols while she does her hair, and the room smells like that Aussie product, and that warm, metallic smell that curling irons get, and you're thinking about dip-dyeing the ends of your hair pastel pink, but you're not sure you can justify the cost of Manic Panic when you just bought distressed magenta jeans at Forever 21, and in your bag you find Crackle nail polish, and you all laugh about how immature you *used* to be, while you pass around the tub of chocolate chip cookie dough that you're taking scoops from with a communal spoon, and everyone has a mission for the night, of someone they're gonna flirt with, or someone they're gonna avoid, or someone they're gonna make jealous via Snapchat, but you all agree you're gonna meet up at that late-night takeout place, and you're actually gonna get it this time, no matter how long you have to wait, and before you head out, you take a selfie together, and you flash a peace sign, and you cover it with a hazy filter called Valencia, and you might not remember anything from this night, but you *will* remember that blurry, square photo of you and the people you were young with.

Some Types Of People I Like

Loudmouths, lesbians who belong to vegetable co-ops, boomer dads who are still in a band, people who collect large plastic jugs to reuse and fill with odds and ends, kind yet rebellious high school English teachers, ukulele chicks, people who have a signature method for preparing a grilled cheese, people who look down and close their eyes and chuckle warmly at the absurdity of it all, people who make kitschy little objects out of clay, people who Slack message you an upside down smiley face when something is annoying at work out of solidarity, self-published authors, animal rights activists, socialist grandmas, modest triathletes, grifters who are self-aware about it, people who own a harp or a loom or a flour grinding mill, fat girls who dress twee, Christians who speak out against Trump, people who wear unflattering or unnaturally colored lipstick (especially if that's the only makeup they wear), people with incredibly strong opinions about cleaning supplies, raggedy children on bikes who engage passersby, Elizabeths, people who would offer you snacks out of a tote bag, certified preowned chill brahs, and Etsy witches.

Lawn Chairs Under The Stars

What are we wearing this summer? We're *wearing* the scent of last night's bonfire still lingering in our hair. Because we fell asleep way too late. After sitting around in a circle of lawn chairs under the stars. With people we love so much that we don't know if our throats are hoarse from the smoke, or from laughing so hard when someone tried and failed to explain the complicated rules of a card game to an audience of people with foam koozies in their hands.

We're *watching* fireworks popping off from an event in the distance. And acknowledging that they're inconsiderate and wasteful. But still feeling a little bit of childlike wonder at the grand finale, when they sizzle, one after the other, and fill the sky with blasts of purple and green and red, and then fade like the embers in the fire pit and the lightning bugs pulsing.

We're *eating* kebabs with lightly blackened edges. Straight off the grill. And molten marshmallows, shimmied off a stick onto a graham cracker. And peaches that taste like candy and drip down to our elbows.

We're *listening* to a crowd singing "bum bum bum" during the chorus of an old song. And the fizz of sparklers against a black sky. And the swish of a hammock swaying in the breeze. And the clink of metal caps popping off glass bottles.

And the same tired, old stories we've already heard a hundred times from the same tired, old people we'll never get tired of.

Santa Monica Boulevard

I don't know what heaven could offer me, because I've woken up in his t-shirt, and we've parallel parked in front of the coffee shop in Silver Lake, and I've leaned on his shoulder in line to pick up two bagel sandwiches wrapped in foil, and one cup of jasmine green tea and one cup of gunpowder.

And we've taken Santa Monica Boulevard the whole way down so we can watch the city wake up through our open windows, and we've parked at the library, and we've walked to the promenade, and down to the pier, and down to the water, and all the way to Venice and back. And we've watched the passersby on roller blades, and the stoners on stairs, and the orange-robed Hare Krishnas, and we've paid cash for vertical-cut hunks of watermelon and mango and honeydew.

And we've wondered who we'd be if we went to different colleges, or followed better advice, but we've concluded that any number of heartbreaks or failures that brought us to this concrete path across the sand with our fingers intertwined was more than worth it. And we've wondered what we'd be in ten years, but we've never questioned who we'd be those things with.

And we've stayed until the sun sets peach, and the Ferris wheel lights up blue, and the streetlights make the palm trees glow, and we've played country music on the freeway. And I've felt the breath catch in my chest as I've watched his wedding ring reflect the passing headlights and flicker as he drums on the steering wheel.

Cinnamon Nutmeg Allspice Ginger Cloves

Consider this. Damp sidewalk, crunchy leaves, high-level clouds; red and orange and brown and gold; cinnamon, nutmeg, allspice, ginger, cloves; big sweatshirt over hands, hint of cologne, thermal socks; apple picking, mulled cider, lattice-top pie; pumpkin patch, pop the top, slippery seeds plinking in the bowl; hot shower, early nightfall, whistling wind; black velvet dress, opaque tights, lace-up boots; *evermore*, *Rumours*, *Harvest Moon*; parsley, sage, rosemary, and thyme; steamy soup pot, pull-apart rolls, tangy cranberry marmalade; radiator heat, three-wick soy candle, throw pillows; *Gilmore Girls* DVD box set, shuffle Scrabble tiles, rehash the past; winged corkscrew, cheese and crackers, assorted tiny candy bars; thin blanket under the duvet, moisturizer, flannel pants; tabletop lamp, paperback thriller, pebble ice water; blurry streetlights through the haze through the sheer curtains; fogging windows, loud rain, dream-filled sleep.

Jeopardy! Tournament of Champions

"I never see you at the club."

Okay, I never see you at the *Jeopardy! Tournament of Champions* viewing party in my living room, while I'm making dinner, and I present to you the Trader Joe's vegan orange chicken morsels and say, "Trader Joe really put his whole tradussy into this one," and you say, "What is tradussy?" and I say, "You're on the board!" implying you were answering a *Jeopardy!* question.

I never see you and your friends going to Michaels in May to buy all the Christmas village houses on clearance, and a bunch of acrylic paints and glitter, and setting up a whole station with butcher paper on the table, and then by the time you have it ready, you're all too tired to paint the tiny fir trees.

I never see you coming back home to watch that video of Jeremy Jordan singing "It's All Coming Back To Me Now," or Jonathan Groff doing "Anything Goes," or, in low moments, Ariana Grande and Seth MacFarlane doing "Suddenly Seymour" in a car.

I never see you reading a Donna Tartt novel in the bath for four hours, adding more hot water with your foot on the faucet repeatedly, and then having to take a whole shower afterwards, because you never actually got clean, you just sat around in still water, and then you have to sit on the bed for twenty minutes to catch your breath because you're overheated.

Where are you there, huh?

Chocolate Lava Cakes

Stop romanticizing everything? That's gonna be hard, because every once in a while, there are chocolate lava cakes baked in ramekins, dusted with powdered sugar, and savored with a tiny teaspoon. And bursts of white, blue, and green hydrangeas spilling over the top of a crystal vase that casts rainbows on the table when the sun hits just right.

And the chord progressions in old Motown songs, and catching someone's eye at the exact second they start to laugh, and streets lined with trees that stretch high above the houses and create a canopy of leaves across the sky.

And a little girl who wants to wear a Halloween dress every single day because she feels such joy twirling around in it. And black ink pens that glide like paint, and wind chimes swaying and playing the notes of a favorite song just by chance, and watermelon slice rinds on a paper plate.

And a VHS that you've returned to since childhood that warbles and shakes, but still plays, and smells like film tape and thick plastic, and an old friend's house somehow.

And walking on the beach with someone you love, and your feet are sinking into the sand, and when you look behind you, you see your footprints side by side, and it looks like a work of art, and you're struck by the knowledge that an uncountable number of humans have done this same thing, in this same place, and felt about it this same way.

World Market

This is what I want, okay? I want to drive to my best friend's house. I want to play *SOS* by SZA. I want to watch her dance down her driveway while I scootch a bunch of trash out of the passenger seat. I want to get two lattes and two pastries. I want her to elbow me out of the way to try to pay for them while I say "nice try" and tap my card. I want her to call me a derogatory word for having done so.

I want to drive to World Market. I want to touch every item in that store. I want to say "this is cute, this is cute, this is cute, that's really cute, that looks like you." I want to have a complex, nuanced conversation about capitalism and consumerism and the battle between our animal desire to gather and our empathy-driven desire to fill the landfills less, and I want to have this conversation while holding salt and pepper shakers that look like croissants.

I want her to say that she needs dog food. I want to accompany her to a second location to buy dog food. I want to be standing in a dog food aisle, having a life-changing conversation about our worst traumas, that seamlessly transitions into listing everything we remember from MTV's *The Real World*.

I want to talk about our families. I want to talk about our mutual friends. I want to talk about our haircuts. I want to talk about whether or not we should wallpaper the downstairs bathroom because the space around the medicine cabinet's gonna be hard and you're probably gonna move next summer, is it really even gonna be worth it?

I want to listen eagerly as she tells me everything she ate last week. This is what I want.

All Of The Tens

I'm waking up at 8:36 AM, I'm making an enormous Belgian waffle with blueberries inside and a cup of black tea, I'm having that on the couch. I'm going for a long run while listening to a chatty podcast like Celebrity Memoir Book Club.

I'm taking a delicious shower where I do everything, the deep conditioner, the skincare. I'm putting on a cute dress with a lace bralette and I'm doing my makeup for fun. I'm going to a coffee shop where I'm getting three shots of espresso in a latte until I'm vibrating out of my skin. I'm reading a book on my phone.

I'm going to a local bookstore, where I'm browsing for titles to request from my library app, while also buying something to support the small business, like a postcard and a buttery pen and a magazine from the 1920s. I'm taking those to a park bench. I'm reading the magazine, I'm captivated by how different people were, but also how the same. I'm writing a letter with those findings to a friend, I'm mailing it to her as a little surprise.

I'm coming back home. I'm making an elaborate salad that requires way too many steps, like roasting chickpeas, and whipping dressing with a fork. I'm watching movies I've seen 100,000 times before, *How To Lose A Guy In 10 Days*, *10 Things I Hate About You*, all of the tens. I'm watching those until I can justify ordering food I wouldn't normally pay for.

I'm sitting on that couch until I'm cozy in bed at 11:15. I'm counting on all ten fingers a list of things I'm grateful for, until they comfort me to sleep.

Dandelion Sunburst

Can you believe this? This morning I woke up under a plush, airy, white linen comforter, atop cotton sheets worn to extra softness.

I filled a glass box with steam and clean, pure water— clean enough to *drink* water— set to my preferred temperature, and then I washed my body with textures and scents that I chose from an endless array of options.

Then I looked through thirty shirts to pick the one I felt like wearing today, and the one I picked smelled like a summer breeze, because there's a machine in my house that washes clothes. And then I put pinky-peachy paints on my face, and adorned myself with fine, precious metals created by asteroids and mined from the depths of the earth, just because it's pretty and fun.

And then I created a fire with the twist of my wrist, and poured into a pan white rice from Thailand, plantains from Honduras, black beans from Florida, red bell peppers, red onions, and yellow corn from down the street, and a squeeze of California lime juice on top.

And then I went outside, and I picked a teeny tiny bouquet of things that are technically weeds, in yellow, chartreuse, cyan, and I twisted the stems between my fingertips, and I rubbed some of the pigment of a yellow dandelion sunburst on the back of my hand, just to feel like a little kid.

And then I looked into the eyes— the gray-blue eyes that I love more than any of these things, or any other thing imaginable— and that person said to *me*, "I'm so happy to see you."

A City I've Never Been To Before

I want to spend two days in a city I've never been to before, with no obligations to fulfill there, except, like, maybe a donut shop I saw online that I want to try. I want to be there with someone I never get tired of talking to, walking along bodies of water, through twisty streets, always replacing the little treat in my hand.

First, a coffee from a place with pretty tile floors and a local musician playing acoustic guitar, and then a hunk of sourdough bread from a bustling marketplace full of local flavor, and then a wax paper bag full of roasted nuts that I get from a street cart and eat on the stairs of an old church with beautiful architecture, and then I want something powdered and cream-filled from a vegan bakery that has quirky tip jars that allow me to vote for NSYNC versus Backstreet Boys with my spare change.

I want to go to a museum, and I want to learn something about this city that I didn't know before, like what famous speech happened here, what band is from here, what they used to manufacture here. I want to carry that information with me for the rest of my life, always informing how I view this place.

I want to go to a little comedy show in a black box theater, and I want to follow all the performers in case they get famous one day.

I want to take pictures of bright-colored doors, and weird cars, and funny stickers on telephone poles covered with staples, and selfies with the person I'm sharing these memories with. And I want to go to bed with tired feet and a newfound curiosity for another place I've never been.

Lemon Drop

Unmade bed, discarded dress mountain. Unplugged sink basin flat iron. Creamy pencil tight-line, pigmented glitter lid taps. Open-mouth mascara, elbow balance earrings. Phone, keys, Black Honey. Flamingo-stance ankle strap buckling.

Booth seat coat pile. Metal chopstick noodle tangle. Chili oil, sesame seeds, tiny scallion rings. Fried rice paper, paper lanterns, paper fortune. *Should we trade? You deserve this one.*

Wet pavement neon sign reflections, gibbous moon, smoke clouds. Textured highball glass, toothpick-speared raspberry, mint leaves, open tab. Lean in, sing along, floor spill, *do that again for a photo*. Sarcastic, earnest, effusive, nonsensical. Lemon drop, name drop, mic drop, pop lock and drop, card drop, pin drop.

Half-ass face-wash, top-of-head bun, undershirt dress. Blurry-eyed scroll, low battery, pic exchange. Stovetop popcorn, HBO static, *thanks again* text. Hoarse voice, tired feet, full cup.

Pet Human

If I had a pet human, like if I were another species responsible for the care and keeping of Homo sapiens in captivity, and I did some research on what they need to be happy, I would conclude that what we most want is to go for long walks, eat fruit, talk about the things that interest us, laze around, make art, and help each other. I really like to apply this to my little problems in life.

Why does my body not feel good? I don't know, have you not gone for a walk? Have you not lazed around? *Why am I not enjoying this email job?* I don't know, are you talking about things that interest you and making art? *Why can't I stop eating or drinking this?* I don't know, does it share any qualities with an overripe mango? Your little animal brain just wants to, and that's fine.

We set all these arbitrary obstacles for ourselves to stop being happy, but at the end of the day, are you helping people? Are you going to get some fruit for the people who can't get the fruit? Are you finding a way to carry someone with you who can't go for a long walk? I just think we should treat ourselves like pets.

Backseat Of An Uber

Summer's not actually over, and there's still time to bury your friend's legs in the sand and turn them into mermaid fins, and to jump underwater and shout and guess what each other said, and to drink something sugary from a carved-out pineapple, and to kiss someone who smells like coconut and aloe, and to connect deeply with a friend-of-a-friend you never thought you had anything in common with under the haze of glowing string lights, and to order Taco Bell at the drive-thru and eat it in a dark corner of the parking lot with way too much hot sauce, and to crack open peanut shells between your thumb and your knuckle and lick the salt off, and to Venmo neighborhood kids for powdered lemonade in a Solo cup, and to watch a budding musician in the park and leave five dollars in their guitar case, and to invite friends over for a hangout that's supposed to last an hour but turns into watching *Shrek* and making brownie mix at 1 AM, and to paint your nails the color of a lawn flamingo, and to wear sunglasses more often than you wear a bra, and to read a romance novel with your bare feet in the grass, and to dip pretzel bites into stone-ground mustard at a rooftop bar and then sit in the backseat of an Uber and listen to Erykah Badu and watch the streetlights blur through the city as you catch a whiff of late August air, which always fills you with a pang of nostalgia for the beginning of a new school year, and makes you feel like anything is possible, and you could be anyone you want to be.

Oath Of Cringe

I will be cringe. I will be corny. I will flop. I will make jokes that people find cheesy, I will make jokes that people find mean, and I will make jokes that people can't find the meaning in. I will say things the wrong way, I will say things that people have already said, and I might say things that nobody needed to say.

I will look ugly. I will look awkward. I will look embarrassing. I will give people who wish me ill fodder to make fun of me.

But I will not not try. I will not sit in the back and nurse my bitter belief that my unrealized ideas are better than someone else's finished product. I will not end my race on this planet grateful that I didn't waste any of my dignity on a business that didn't pan out, or a relationship that didn't last forever, or a book that nobody bought, or a video that nobody watched. I will not wait to be thinner or prettier or older. I will not hold onto the belief that I missed my boat when I was thinner or prettier or younger.

I would rather tell an embarrassing story of vulnerability and bravery than a flattering story of comfort and nothing.

I will be the flop who tried it all. I will be the flop who drank every last drop. I will be the flop who felt every feeling.

Part 2

Going In

"Never go with a hippie to a second location."

—Jack Donaghy, *30 Rock*

Show Dog

One day you'll be scrolling, and you'll come across an amateur eugenicist analyzing a woman's appearance like she's a show dog, talking about the color of her eyes, and the shape of her teeth, and the curve of her jaw, and using sci-fi villain language to ascribe a numerical value to her beauty, placing on a scale from one to ten the unfathomable gorgeousness of a creature born of thousands of years of love, and hate, and passion, and boredom, and sacrifice, all made out of the same stardust that made the mountains, and the clouds, and the trees, and then he'll say that her nose is flat, or that her lips are mid, and you'll think about how every person who has ever felt a feeling was grown inside a warm belly, and carried in arms, and fed through the night, and then you'll feel a sinking rock of pity in your stomach, that any one of these scientific wonders could feel so betrayed, and so rejected, that his hurt is on a rampage, squashing in its fist the awe of human beauty, until it fits his scale from one to ten. And then you'll think, more likely than not, he will blame those who consider his pain more than those who don't. And then you'll keep scrolling.

Everything You've Ever Wanted

I just think you're gonna get everything you've ever wanted in life. I just have a really strong feeling about that. I just think that one of these days, you're gonna wake up in a world where you have the relationships that you want and deserve, and you'll feel totally at peace with them.

And you're gonna go to the job that's such a perfect fit for you that it never really feels that hard, but you get the satisfaction of putting in the effort. And you're gonna get paid the amount of money that you need to retain the motivation to get out of bed, but you'll never have to make decisions based around money. You'll be able to leave any situation that's not serving you, you'll be able to get anything that would make your life better, and you'll have the resources to do so.

And I think you're gonna have the kinds of relationships where you can call so many people, at any hour of the day, and they will want to do things for you, because you add so much value to their lives that they'll be eager for an opportunity to give it back to you.

And I think that you're gonna have time to just feel pleasure, and appreciate the things that you love, and notice new things that you love all the time, because you're gonna have all of your basic needs met. And you're gonna have all that free energy to feel good.

I just have a feeling that this is what's gonna come to you. I could be wrong… but I don't think that I am.

Roadmap

Were you aware that sometimes there are cardboard crates full of roadside farmstand strawberries, so ripe and so plump that they melt on your tongue, while you ride in the passenger seat, with your feet on the dash, and let the radio scan, until it lands on an Eagles song that transports you to a different time and place?

And were you aware that there are Pacific Coast Highways with Santa Monica mountains on one side and ocean foam at the other, and burnt orange and lilac desert mesas that seem like they're under a spotlight of the sun, and infinite plains that make you notice the hugeness of the sky, and rolling green hills dappled with pink milkweed, feeding monarch butterflies that migrate 2,000 miles home, even after feeling paradise on their tiny wings?

And were you aware that sometimes there are red brick buildings half consumed by vines, and skyscrapers with hundreds of lives happening simultaneously, stacked atop each other, behind a sheet of glass?

And were you aware that sometimes there are unremarkable houses in rusted towns, with nothing to show for themselves except for the sticky, laminated pages of a heavy, faded photo album that serves as a roadmap of your life, and an old chair that contours like it remembers you, and a person who makes you green tea and watches you grow?

Brunch Debriefing

If you have somebody in your life with whom you would totally want to eat brunch for an hour and a half, and then take a brunch debriefing walk, where you discuss everything you just discussed in further detail while moving…

and if you have somebody who would totally sit on the floor with you while you fold laundry, and listen to every rambling thought in your inner monologue…

and if you have somebody with whom you would totally want to ride around while they're picking up medicine at the drive-thru, or getting their dry cleaning, and you would want to hear every thought they've ever had…

and if you have somebody who has either been there for so many events in your history, or has heard about them so many times, that it feels like there's another set of eyes looking back on your life, and you can totally discuss every character because they know you so deeply…

and if there's somebody who, if you went missing, the cops could call and get a totally minute-by-minute play-by-play of everything that's ever happened to you…

and if you have somebody who could totally look at a list of a thousand options for food or clothes or something and know what you would pick?

Cherish them. Priceless.

Easter Sunday

Easter Sunday is a weird one, because I grew up very religious, and now I don't know. I'm devoid of answers. I don't even know how to approach finding answers.

But I do know that today I watched a horde of little kids throw their entire bodies into chasing after a butterfly because they wanted one more glimpse of it.

And today I sat on the driveway and I looked up at three different trees that were all starting to bloom, and one was a really saturated yellow, and one was a really pale pink, and one was a really vibrant green, and they were all mixing together from my vantage point to look like an impressionist painting, but it wasn't a painting, it was what I was seeing with my eyes.

And today I heard this vocal harmony that required four very talented people to weave their voices together to create an incredible sound that none of them could have made on their own.

And today I ate a fruit salad that was a ripe mix of raspberries and strawberries and blackberries and blueberries and kiwis, all layered in a deep glass bowl, and it was made for me by a person who, very recently, I was not at all confident would be here today.

I don't know anything, but I do know those things.

Be 22

It's come to my attention that you're not 22. What are you doing to address this? The men in power want to see 22. They've made this clear. There are studies and sciences and charts and environmentalist private jet-owning celebrities in their 50s to back this up. It's what they want. It's what they deserve. Please give it to them.

If you're under 22, please age yourself up. If you are 22, please begin anti-aging to maintain it. If you're older than 22, make it a hobby. You can probably stretch it for another ten years, and after that, you're going to have to go full time. People aren't going to believe you're 22, but it is still a requirement that you want to be.

I don't want to hear any of your excuses. None of your "oh, I would be so heartbroken to hear a grandmother say that she spent her whole life pursuing aging backwards," or "oh, I would never look into the eyes of a little girl and tell her to map out her life to suit the interests of random men." None of your "I like to customize my body for fun," or your "my partner likes me the way I am," or your "I'm not trying to win the approval of others."

This isn't about you. It's about 22. Be 22.

Home Library

Oh, she's complicated? I feel like she's been pretty clear in her desire for a four-story home library with finely bound books lining dark wood, ornately carved shelves, with gliding ladders, and massive picture windows framing evergreen trees (swaying in a rainstorm), and armchairs facing the glow of a red brick fireplace.

If you want to get technical about it, she might also enjoy some intriguing old portraits, and celestial maps, and antique atlases in gold frames (with downward casting spotlights). And some glass-front cabinetry full of worldly curiosities, like busts carved in marble, and delicate dried flowers, and (haunted?) crystal balls.

And, if you need to, maybe a little reading nook, with throw pillows piled high, in different fabrics and textures (some tufted velvet, some oversized and soft, some with artisan beading and embroidery), and, like, a little end table with a steaming hot porcelain teapot (and dark chocolate truffles).

And like, she's not going to be *mad* about a spiral staircase, leading up to the domed skylight, that spreads shadows down onto the heirloom rug-covered hardwood by day, and through which you can see every star at night.

And if you can manage to be leaning against the wall (in a tailored linen shirt), to announce that the personal chef is ready with the (candlelit, violin-serenaded) dinner, so be it.

24-Hour Diner

Nothing is ever gonna hit quite the same as being a teenager with a best friend and a summer break with nowhere to go and nothing to do. Except for walk circles around Walmart until the employees start to glare at you. And buy a half gallon tub of off-brand cookies and cream ice cream, and two flimsy metal spoons. And eat it while loitering at the top of the playground stairs.

And then you roll around in the grass, and then you lie on top of one of those metal picnic tables with the little holes that leave marks on your skin, and then you put your heads together, and then you stare up at the sky, and then you talk about all the people you know, and your scary (but exciting) (and rapidly approaching) adult lives, until the sky starts to fade, from blue to sunsetty pink, and gives way to that glowy orange, and the humidity gives way to the early nighttime chill.

So you drive around, and you listen to mix CDs, or maybe you call the local radio station to request "I Got A Feeling" by Black Eyed Peas, and you end up at the 24-hour diner, where there's no one around except for the waitress who always takes pity on you, because she knows, between the two of you, you only have a five-dollar bill to spend. But she keeps bringing you fresh cups of tea, knowing you're gonna leave a three-dollar tip.

And you talk and you talk and you talk, and you think you might run out of things to talk about, but you never do. Because this is your person, and you own the world together.

Overcast

What if you wake up on a gray, overcast day and decide to go to the beach anyway? And it's one of those beaches where you can see for miles on end in three directions, or actually four, if you count the sky, which is particularly huge today, because the cloud coverage is helping you see where the sun is filtering through and where it isn't?

And you walk to the edge of the water, and you feel that salty tingle on your ankles, and then your shins, and then your thighs, and you're thinking that the seagulls are quite pretty today, because their gray and white is blending together perfectly with the sky and the ocean, and you're tracing that line where the two meet with your eyes, and you're thinking, *Wow, I really can't see the other side of this ocean.*

In fact, the extent to which I can't see it is kind of unfathomable, which means I definitely can't fathom the size of the continent I live on.

Which means I certainly can't fathom the size of the planet I live on.

Which means don't even get me started on the size of the sun.

But now the sun is starting to shine down on you more. The clouds are parting, and your thoughts fade back to the here and now. So you stretch your arms out wide, and you do a dorky little spin, because it's hard to be self-conscious when the only other people here, on this bad beach day, are an elderly couple holding hands, and a parent experiencing the earth for the first time again through the eyes of their laughing child, and a few people just like you, standing alone, against the gray-blue, feeling similarly small and awestruck.

Favorite Raindrop

I'm actually a fortune teller, and I saw a day in your future that feels a little bit like waking up without an alarm, when your body is rested and ready, and the first delicate sip of a latte in a circular mug with lightly steamed oat milk poured right up to the rim.

And walking next to fresh jasmine growing along a trellis, and holding one perfumey star in your palm, and light filtering through a stained-glass window to paint the sidewalk magenta and turquoise, and the first bite through the taut skin of a Honeycrisp apple, and nowhere to be for hours and hours.

And then it's all airy, jewel-tone chiffon that swishes gently when you walk, and a wispy gold chain around your wrist, and gold bubbles racing to the top of a long neck flute, and a tiny corner table in a restaurant by the glow of a tiny lamp.

And then it feels like marveling at the intricate details in an old theater ceiling, and lacing your fingers together into the hand of someone you trust, and an orchestra kicking up and filling the air and filling your chest.

And then it's all resting your forehead against a car window on a long drive, and picking your favorite raindrop and watching it slip out of sight, and slipping off your heels, and sinking your foot pads into carpet. And then it feels like melting under the weight of black sleep.

Sexy Achilles Tendons

Are the leg bones in your skeleton shaped the hot way or the less hot way? Do you have too much skin on your eyelids or not enough skin on your eyelids? Does your brow bone suggest that people in your lineage had enough access to potatoes, or do you have low-income eyes? Are your hair follicles shaped correctly? Do you have strawberry skin? Do you have pear shape? Do you have grape spleen? Does your canthal tilt tilt the good direction? Do you have the correct cheek to chin ratio? Do you have the correct clavicle to waist ratio? Do you have the correct waist to hip ratio? Do you have the correct pelvis to ankle ratio? Do you have sexy Achilles tendons? Do you have ugly elbows? Do you have Ozempic vulva or fat knees? If you overlaid an image of a mathematically perfect face on an iPad and then contorted your features into the lines, would it be better or worse looking than Jenna Ortega? Am I worthy of love? Is Amazon my god? Are you my mother? Do I have aging lip skin? Do I have tired heart?

Ice Skating Rink

It's a Saturday morning in January. We haven't seen the sun or shaved a leg in many moons, but we wanted to feel like we were in a Hallmark movie, so we've made it through the slush and the gray and the salt and the speckled windshield all the way to the ice skating rink. We are wearing staticky beanies, thick socks, and like three layers of hand cream under our gloves, and we are baby fawns learning to walk on the ice.

Our bodies do not remember the mechanics of this task, but we're emboldened by the playlist of "Teenage Dream" and "Gangnam Style," so around the time they start playing "Fireflies," we find our footing. We start to enjoy the stretch in our legs, and we stop getting lapped by third graders.

We smell sugar in the air and remember the entire point of being here is actually stale mini marshmallows, in watery hot chocolate, out of paper cups. We savor that— it's technically terrible, but couldn't be better— and then we make our way out into the biting wind.

We take off our hats because we're quite flushed from the exercise, and we take a selfie. Just beige sky, beige concrete, and two colorful, laughing freaks who make each other infinitely happy.

We spend the rest of the day in couch mode at your house. We yelp when we pop a spoon into a can of cinnamon rolls, and we bake that alongside some breakfast casserole I've wanted to try with celery and garlic and onion and rosemary and thyme. We eat off of fine china plates in front of Sofia Coppola's *Marie Antoinette,* and then we switch to a reality show we can talk over for hours.

We wear old sweats, beat dead horses, share old stories, drink hot tea, and make new memories in our own little insulated snow globe.

Okay, One More

Following the sound of your friends' laughter to the back corner of the restaurant. The part of the ice cream sandwich that sticks to your finger pads, scraping it off with your teeth. Wearing your mom's old brown leather purse. Everyone's bathing suits dangling together from the shower curtain rod.

Plinking a fingernail against a wine glass, tilting it side to side in the light. Stirring the soup and tapping the wooden spoon on the edge of the Dutch oven, clang-clang. Sliding gemstones on a bracelet that you pretend have magical properties, or maybe do. Her text vibrating your bedside table, she got home safe, thank you for the lovely night.

The moment your screwdriver lifts the metal lid off the paint can. Tchaikovsky's Pas de Deux from *The Nutcracker*. A stack of library books with yellowed pages and laminated dust covers. That photo of your dad that looks just like you.

Pulling a hot cookie in two and puzzle-piecing the halves together again. Waiting for the church bells to chime the time, too engrossed in each other to check phones. Breathing in the smell of his sweater.

Different colors of light illuminating the apartment complex windows at night. Heeled boots that zip up your calves and leave exclamation point prints on the snow. When you have to leave, really you do, but they're playing our song now... okay, one more.

Screening

After a grueling day on medium screen, when I feel like I'm gonna scream, I like to little screen while I big screen, you know what I mean? I do gym routine on gym machine, prop up little screen on medium gym machine screen, eavesdrop on all the little screens. I think about getting a wrist screen, or maybe the reading screen without the sheen.

If I really need a break, I drive to huge screen, catch a screening, put little screen in my pocket and come out feeling serene, drive with music on car screen, work up an appetite for more little screen.

If little screen isn't little screening, sometimes I'll split screen little screen, watch two little screen things on one little screen, and then I'll just screen screen screen-screen, blast the delicate lacework of synapses in my animal brain that evolved to gather berries with more information than it can possible process and then google "benzodiazepine," screen screen screen, screen, sit next to my partner while we both little screen, and we have big screen in between to set the scene, and then if anyone calls, I'll just screen.

Cast Iron Tub

What does a girl have to do to be submerged in a deep, white, cast iron tub, next to a cracked-open window, with the water perfectly hot and the outdoor evening summer breeze perfectly cool?

Like just under dim, warm, yellow lights, surrounded by thick, glowing candles and fragrant eucalyptus? Only listening to the sounds outside, usually crickets chirping, or the wind blowing, or the hoot of a train whistle in the far distance? But with sporadic bouts of conversation, and dogs barking, and laughter, and cars whooshing by filled with music and people enjoying their night together?

What's a girl have to do to have her muscles perfectly relaxed and stretched in a sprinkle of Epsom salt, freshly exfoliated and cleansed? After a long day of milling about, popping into shops, and having long conversations on a long path, under a canopy of bright green trees with pops of wildflowers in purple and orange and yellow?

Like what does she have to be doing to get an ice cold water with cucumber and lemon and mint? With her pores opening from the steam, and the remainder of her makeup from the day smudging and blurring in a way that's uniquely beautiful, but for her benefit only?

And then stepping out of the tub, into the embrace of an oversized, soft towel, and smothering her body in moisturizing cream, and slipping into a slinky nightgown and a silky robe?

And then diving into bed with a book? And like whatever hurt she carries in her body, or in her heart, is on pause, if only for this moment?

Art Museum

I have this craving today that I feel like could only be satisfied by low humidity, 80 degrees, dew-damp green grass, going for a silent, space-out run, drinking cold water in a hot shower.

And then linen dress, sandals, claw clip, sunglasses, OPI Funny Bunny, blood orange mimosa with a zest garnish, plump raspberries, hash browns, scramble, thick slice of airy sourdough toast with butter and blackberry preserves, peoplewatching, little thrift shop, new cardigan, iced latte with a sprinkle of brown sugar, pain au chocolat, the Mamas and the Papas on the way to the art museum.

And then arm slid around my waist, voice next to my ear, Which painting speaks to you in this room? Me too, I can't stop looking at it, that moss green next to that red. What would you call that, vermillion? I read that both of those pigments were really toxic. I wonder if they knew what they had when they saw this. I wonder if they knew how many people would have to work together to keep it safe for us to see it now. I love the way you think, Stevie Wonder on the drive home.

And then stretchy pants, oversized sweatshirt on the couch, Wikipedia deep-dive into the artists' life stories, the first two thirds of *Titanic*, he makes fun of it and I laugh and then switch to old jazz standards, cook dinner as the sun sets, crusty bread drenched in olive oil and balsamic vinegar, I do the salad, you do the pasta, we do the rest of our lives together always looking for the decadence in the everyday.

Part 3
In And Out

"Some random quote from *Lord of the Rings*, incorrectly attributed to Martin Luther King."

—Bo Burnham, *Inside*

Touch Grass

Get off my phone and go touch grass? When has grass ever shown me what fruit would look like if it were made out of glass and you cut it in half? When has grass ever put a bunch of glitter on a makeup brush and swirled it around in front of my eyes? When has grass ever shown me what hot girls look like lip syncing to Sabrina Carpenter songs?

When has grass ever given me a terrible opinion on a literary fiction novel, or recommended to me self-published books about mermaids gentle-domming sea monsters? When has grass ever taught me how to boil tofu so that more salt gets in the little crevices?

When has grass ever taught me how to day trade SPY options? When has grass ever shown me the same piece of jewelry 100,000 times until I finally relent and order it and then by the time it arrives I wish I hadn't bought it?

When has grass done that for me? When has grass… my attention span is too short to finish this.

I Know What I'm Working With

I'm not ugly, and you won't be able to convince me that I'm ugly. Sorry. I had a post go viral talking about men, and the 99% who've experienced flirting, got the joke. The 1% remaining is trying to hit me with "You're an uggo."

Guess what? It may have worked when I was 17, may have worked when I was 22. But I'm 34, baby. I'm in the sweet spot between youthful beauty and womanly confidence, and I know what I'm working with.

I have no illusions. This is not for everyone. Not everyone's cup of tea. I went to a state college full of normie bros, and it did not get a lot of play. However, I've been around long enough to know exactly who I *am* for.

Dungeon Masters: love me.

Gen X guys scanning the party for someone to explain ska music to: target audience.

Autistic lesbians with really intense stares but very good intentions: I'm your original Midwest Princess.

Bisexual men with facial piercings who've tried tripping Robitussin: kryptonite.

Pedantic scholars of niche topics: tell me more, professor.

The guys who work at Valvoline. I don't know why with that one, but 100% success rate.

So if you're gonna try to tell me that I'm ugly, first come see the way they look at me when they show me the little stick with the oil on it.

I know what I'm working with.

Text Post

Optimism

Wearing a tank top the first time it's over 50 degrees has the same energy as deciding your period's over despite evidence to the contrary, and I call that stone-cold bloody optimism.

Em Dash

It's gross that em dashes look like AI now— they're the most poetic punctuation mark?? We should start using them even more— in contexts where they don't strictly— make sense— just Emily Dickinson ourselves out of this mess—

Hamilton

I think I'm not that threatened by AI art because *Hamilton* isn't great because it rhymes. It's great because some freaking weirdo read a biography on a plane and had to rap about it. Humans are so weird, and so inevitably so, and we want more of each other, and we can't help it.

Twilight

Did anyone else go through this with *Twilight?* Where you were like, "yeah, it's good, I like it."

But then you were like, "but the story's bad and the writing's bad, so it's bad," but then you were like, "but it has this massive following, this huge impact— can it really be bad?" but then you were like, "well, do we want to define art based off of how many people like it?"

But then you were like, "well, why do we hold things girls like to such high standards? Why is it frivolous just because it's feminine? We don't do that for boys," but then you were like, "But it's not good for young girls to look up to this character who's so weak."

But then you were like, "that's pretty condescending to young girls, especially ones who love to read, to think they're not going to engage critically with the material," but then you were like, "but stories really shape our culture, and this character defines herself based off of men," but then you were like, "well, why have we gotten to the point of devaluing marriage and motherhood so much that it's inherently weak? That's misogynistic."

But then you were like, "have I ever spent this much time thinking about pop fiction written by a man? Is it possible that *Twilight* is… perfect?"

No, it's not. But Kristen Stewart is really beautiful.

This Might Be Weird

This might be weird, but do you want to hang out sometime? This might be weird, but do you want to stay for lunch? This might be weird, but do you want to stay indefinitely?

This might be weird, but do you want to show me how you see the world? This might be weird, but do you want to unzip your hurts and let me dig around inside? This might be weird, but do you want to pass your secrets down to me like family recipes?

This might be weird, but do you want to go out tonight? This might be weird, but do you want to stay in? This might be weird, but do you want to always be my most recent text? This might be weird, but do you want to be weird together?

This might be weird, but I already fell in love. Do you want to come down here and join me in it?

Aristocats

I don't think we need to have billionaires, but I'm okay with Aristocats.

I'm not opposed to wealth in general. If you create something valuable, you're great at business, you're great at art, you invent something important, then sure, reap some benefits for you and your family. Just reap those benefits by enjoying the pleasures of life and trying to help as many other people do so as possible.

Be an Aristocat. Spend your days playing piano, painting with your hands, strolling the streets of Paris, getting seduced by a roué hanging out of a tree and going to his rooftop apartment to watch his friends play jazz accordion. Befriend a drunk goose. Coquettishly strum a harp.

What are you doing instead? You're running out every small business until people are starving? You're trying to own human beings? You're digging holes in the earth that will eventually swallow us all whole, you're shooting pop stars into space for five minutes, you're renting Sydney

Sweeney's attendance to your wedding? You're creating bombs? Pathetic. Rich people used to build libraries.

You're one of the few people on this planet who could live like a cartoon cat wearing a bowtie, and instead of practicing your scales and arpeggios, you're dismantling democracy?

Who's Bored Of The Moon?!

There's a huge rock spinning around us?! Always has been, always will be?! It reflects the sun, glows a moody, black-and-white-filmy, 19050s-Christmas-lights kind of glow?!

It makes you feel total awe and wonder at the majesty of being alive?! And every person who's ever perceived anything has also felt that way?! And probably most of the animals?! And maybe the plants?! And it pulls on the ocean and makes the waves?! And it probably controls the fertility systems that make more humanity through our connections with one another?!

And when you look at a full moon on a fall night, and there's dark blue clouds drifting in front of it, it makes you want to write poems?! And it makes you want to write songs?! And we do?! And we always have?! And we always will?! And we never get sick of it?!

You can think some art is boring, but who's bored of the moon?! Nobody's bored of the moon!

For You Page

Forearms

I'm so mad that Reddit told men that women like it when they roll up the sleeves of their dress shirts. Now they're all peacocking around with their forearms out. You can't tell who means it in an understated, genuine, kind of Greg Kinnear way, and who's being a dirty little harlot. It's like when Bill Hader found out he was hot and it ruined the whole thing. Steve Kornacki sashaying in front of that map. They can't handle this information. Stop telling them. For every Adam Scott, you get a Chris Pratt.

Musk

Wannabe king of the world has everything gold-plated, and his name literally means "to win in a showboaty manner," and his supervillain crony has a chin implant and a name that literally means "the sometimes alluring and sometimes repulsive scent of masculinity." If this were a prestige drama everyone was talking about, I would feel superior to it, and I would mock it for the characters' names being too on the nose.

Flamingo

You'll never be able to hurt my feelings, because one time I was wearing pink shorts and a pink shirt, and a car full of teenagers drove by and yelled, "It's a flamingo!" And I'm not a flamingo. And it stung.

It's Probably Fine

It's probably fine, right, that the website that used to be a marketplace for handmade crafts and gifts is now mostly AI generated images dropshipped on single-use or useless plastic, right?

And it's probably fine that the website that used to be for collecting inspiration for DIY projects and fashion and home decor is now mostly an algorithm that determines what you would want to see and then generates those images with AI to approximate what they would look like in real life, right?

And it's probably fine that people are incentivized to create content that's controversial, whether it be cruel or false, and it's probably fine that we call things that artists make "content" and that that's the same word we apply to things that AI makes? And ads?

And it's probably fine that mushy brains can get fed one video after another on a topic until they fall deep into an echo chamber that convinces them to hate people, people of any kind of group, right? That's probably good?

And it's probably good that we all joke about how we hate hanging out, hate answering the phone, hate going places, hate keeping plans, hate talking? That's all good, right?

I'm not hopeless about the world, I'm not hopeless about the internet— I can't be— but sometimes you just have to ask... is it fine?

Boomers

Things that feel like they belong to Baby Boomers, from a millennial: panty hose, lead, cottage cheese, owning houses, tipping 15%, grayscale children saying "why I oughtta!" while wielding wooden bats, vaseline, tying cardigans around their shoulders, wall-to-wall carpet, smoking in cars, answering the phone when they can't talk right now, timeshares, canned fruit, boiled vegetables, going steady, rum raisin, figs, saying that they don't care if someone is "white or black or green or purple," mailing articles cut out of newspapers, savings bonds, forever stamps, memes of the Minions that look like they've been screenshot and reposted fifteen times and then thrown into a bath tub also containing a toaster, bathroom scales, patriotism, convertibles, lawn sprinklers, celery, metal folding chairs, listening to someone describe a baseball game on an AM/FM radio, crossing their legs at the ankle, using ellipses in an inscrutable manner, sharing a milkshake with two straws, Jimmy Buffet's chain restaurant, tomato juice, and that novelty wall plaque of a fish that sings Bobby McFerrin songs.

Gen X

Things that feel like they belong to Gen X, from a millennial: food courts, petitions, the phrase "bent out of shape," breast implants, canned food drives, bumper stickers, tater tots and to a lesser extent potato chips, printers, Q-tips, recycling, highlighters and staplers, Ulta Beauty, body lotion in a bottle with a pump, pink plastic disposable razors, the birth control pill, bands, saying the line "what happened to you, man?" in a movie, reading a whole article, tilting everything in their Instagram story on its side, volleyball, half iced tea and half lemonade, talking on the phone but not in public, hand sanitizer, bringing a guitar to a bonfire, posters, ordering fish at a restaurant, helium balloons, the rumor that Barack Obama and Jennifer Aniston are hooking up, Styrofoam, metal orthodontic braces, swimming in lakes, yellow and green kitchen sponges with one side that's abrasive, basements, also cinder block in general, yogurt, driving with the windows down, gas stations, and grapes.

Millennials

"I don't want people to think I'm a millennial!"

Jessica, we're 34. Everyone knows we're millennials. Jason knows it, Emily knows it. We're as millennial as the Urban Decay Naked 2.

You're not a girl, fully a woman. You can pay your automo-bills. We've been through a lot. We know who A is, we know how he met their mother. We don't also want to win a Dundie for "Most in Denial About the Passage of Time." You're being a Carrie. It's time to Miranda up.

So your shoulder tattoo of seagulls taking flight is fading a little bit? That's fine. Josh and Alex were talking the other day, and they said you're trying too hard to stay relevant, and it's a real Heidi situation. So let's be LC. Fix your cat eye, fill your mason jar with La Croix, and accept that we're middle aged.

Gen Z

I love Gen Z. What's not to love? Their elders are afraid of them because they're macabre, and they're ironic, and they wear star-shaped pimple patches in public, and they don't share our same rules for eye contact, and a not insignificant number of them are child Republicans.

But they're also kind, and accepting, and inventive with their cutesy hand gestures, and they don't like fast fashion or factory farming, and they wear AirPods at work so you don't have to make small talk with them while they fix the flashing light on your self-checkout kiosk.

They have a lot of anxiety disorders, and they smoke things with USB ports that taste like caramel cheesecake, and a few of them have sex with holographic images of animated Japanese schoolgirls, sure, but you can say the same for millennials. You can call them phone addicts with no attention spans, but try getting your Silent Generation grandma off of Candy Crush.

The only thing that truly sets Gen Z apart is their ability to face impending doom with a shrug and a wilted flower emoji. The kids are all right.

Writer's Block

Do you ever get writer's block? So you try all your tricks, like you go to a random word generator and you get three words, but now you're just staring at tributary apricot bamboozle, and still nothing's happening?

So then you listen to film scores to try to get in the right mindset, but all you get is in the mood to watch edits of Paul Mescal gazing at people with Celtic eyes of longing?

So then you text a friend who's also a writer and you're like, *Maybe I was never good at this, maybe I never liked this, maybe I should quit this, maybe I should be an electrician*, and they're like, *Probably not, but pop off?*

So then you read a passage from your favorite book, but all it does is remind you that you can't do that, so then you read a passage from a book you hate, but all it does is remind you that that person actually finished theirs?

So then you're like, *Maybe I need a break*, but then you get the song from *Hamilton* stuck in your head, and you start watching a bunch of videos of theatre girls lip syncing with drawn-on Crayola marker beards?

And then you're like, *Maybe I need to try a different artform,* but you're not good at any other artforms, so now you're just a person who's not writing who's also not using all this embroidery floss?

So then you try to go for a walk to shake ideas out, but nothing shakes out, so now you're just sweaty and flushed and confused like a bamboozled apricot tributary?

In Pursuit Of Beauty

I will: put bleach strips on my teeth.
I will not: go to the dentist.

I will: rub flesh-eating acid into my skin to exfoliate it.
I will not: inject my muscles with botulism to paralyze them. (Yet. We'll see about the future.)

I will: watch hundreds of hours of seasonal color analysis videos.
I will not: learn what the hell they're talking about.

I will: melt the hair out of my face with toxic creams.
I will not: learn how to shape my eyebrows.

I will: touch everything in Sephora.
I will not: stop being afraid of the people who work there.

I will: sleep with my hair wrapped around the belt from a robe to curl it.
I will not: sleep with tape over my mouth to do whatever that's supposed to do.

I will: pay someone $300 to change the color of my hair.
I will not: take the requisite steps to maintain it.

I will: keep buying lipstick.
I will not: stop gnawing on my lips like a rabid raccoon.

I will: analyze and critique the patriarchal beauty standards that lead women to feel like they're on a never-ending hamster wheel of consumption, buying more and more products that are designed to make them feel inadequate, to keep them complacent, or dependent on men, or to stall their career progress.
I will not: stop following the Kardashians on Instagram.

For All You Know

For all you know, someone you've walked past a hundred times in a busy blur could one day be the person you call first with good news. For all you know, the project you worked on ten years ago could reach the right eyes and that seed could grow to change your life. For all you know, the compliment you gave someone in passing could be the thing that keeps them hanging on. For all you know, the thing you're sure you hate could one day be your favorite, and the thing you're sure you love could one day warrant a tattoo removal appointment. For all you know, you have so many experiences left to experience. For all you know, there is so much you don't.

Part 4
Falling Out

"Please leave me stranded. It's so romantic."

—Taylor Swift, "New Romantics"

Spare A Thought For Thigh Gaps

Hey, just checking in to make sure you're spending your one unpromised century on this spinning rock full of pleasures and miseries thinking about hip dips? And lip flips? And microdermabrasion and Lipo 360 and the amount of protein equivalent to your weight multiplied by 0.36 in grams and crepe skin and 445cc moderate profile half under the muscle?

Like yes, your existence is the result of ancient atoms rearranging infinitely until they created your unique consciousness that can make art and make love and make jokes and make room in your heart to care about other people with a strength that overpowers even your own desire to live, but if you get around to it, could you please spare a thought for thigh gaps? And bikini bridges? And elevens and crow's feet and marionettes and nasolabial folds?

Sure, you only get one chance to experience the wonders of this planet, but you also only get one chance to wonder whether the hole in your naval carved by a woman sacrificing her selfhood to grow you from scratch is starting to pucker and sag from the gravity that tethers us to it.

Walk-In Closet

Once I have a perfectly organized walk-in closet with floor-to-ceiling white open shelves with cubbies for each pair of shoes and each bag so I can see everything at once…

and there's a rack with wooden hangers displaying my minimalist, curated capsule wardrobe, containing only fine materials tailored to my body that are designed to last a lifetime…

and they're arranged by color and type, so each section begins with my one white t-shirt, my one white blouse, my one white summer dress, my one pair of light-wash jeans, and then some colorful, fun pieces that make my skin glow and show off my style…

and there's also an energy efficient, quiet washing machine, so there's never a hamper, never a pile of folded clothes, and you just open the French doors to the Juliet balcony, where it's always the perfect weather to line-dry everything so that it smells like sun and summer breeze…

and that smell mixes perfectly with my designer makeup, and the expensive hand cream collection that lines the dresser, which also contains my beautiful lingerie collection, which then has a hidden drawer beneath it containing all my jewelry, collected from my extensive travels or gifted to me by admirers?

Then it's over for you.

Tangerine

Tonight I was driving into this massive sunset, and the sky was melting from gray-blue to blush pink to tangerine, and I've always loved that glowy orange of a sunset, but I never thought to call it "tangerine" until I was really impacted by a movie that called it that, and now when I see that color, it's almost like I see it *better*.

And I was listening to music as loudly as I reasonably could, and my hand was a fish out the window, and the bassline was thrumming through my whole body, and it was healing me the way that a cat's purrs heal you. And I always liked music, but I never knew how to listen to bass until a musician friend of mine taught me how to isolate the bassline out and hear what it was doing on its own, and hear what it was doing to support the rest of the music, and now when I hear a song that I've always liked, I almost like it *better*.

And I was thinking about a friend of mine who had a rough day, and feeling so grateful for her, and I was thinking about this compliment she once gave me, when she said that I'm an extremely grateful person. And knowing that someone who loves me sees me that way made me see *myself* that way, and her compliment made me *grateful* to be a grateful person.

I know that all three of these people— the filmmaker, the musician, the friend— were trying to do something impactful, but I don't know if any of them knew that they were permanently altering my inner world and my music and my sunsets.

Dopamine Factory

Am I addicted to my phone? I'm not addicted to my phone.

I *like* to cradle a tiny dopamine factory in my palm that feels silky smooth against my fingertips and lights up and pings like a 24-hour casino while delivering into my brain a constant stream of information designed to elicit an emotional reaction out of me as quickly as possible.

I feel *calmed down* by scrolling past color and motion and sound and more faces than my ancestors would have seen in a lifetime.

It makes me feel like I *accomplished something* to get my heart rate up through an argument with a stranger or through seeing high-definition footage of a tragedy from every possible angle.

It makes me feel *at peace* to have access to a database of every human being who's ever been alive and to see if any of them like me. Someone on one of these apps might be trying to tell me that they love me! Like not on that one, but maybe on that one? Yes! Right there, see? Someone loves me and that feels good. Someone also hates me, but like, they hate me through a phone. I'll just put the phone down because I'm not addicted to a phone.

But there might be something big happening. There might be some kind of historical movement going on, and it would be irresponsible of me to not look. I might be able to ease someone's suffering or bring someone joy or get money get attention get beauty get love get confirmation that I'm worthy of being alive.

I'm not addicted to my phone.

Grief Has Felt Like

Grief has felt like an airport at 5 AM, a dimly lit liminal space where music bounces eerily off tunnel walls, leading to a TV's flashing reminders that the world continues on when you're not awake to see it.

Grief has felt like a vomit, a contraction, a sudden and forceful heave from within your gut that must happen with or without your permission.

Grief has felt like falling to your knees in a crowded city crosswalk, people rushing around in their workout clothes and their work suits, as you're screaming, *It's over! It's over! Why are you all still here?*

Grief has felt like the rote mundanity of leftovers in Tupperware and lint pulled from dryer vents and soap on loofah on body, and it has felt like curiously watching a paper cut split and fill with blood before the pain starts.

Grief has felt like everyone else you love reduced to sitcom rerun stock characters in a never-ending, mind-numbing rhythm of line, line, laugh track.

Grief has felt like why are we learning this? We're never going to use this in real life.

Grief has felt like chipped toenail polish you never remove, just trim away in miniscule crescents, a week at a time.

A State Of Kale Smoothie

Sorry I couldn't answer your call. I was in a state of kale smoothie, B12 gummy, Olaplex bun, Crest White Strips, the Pink Stuff Miracle Power Foaming Toilet Cleaner, Dawn Power Wash, Korean exfoliation mitt, iron the duvet, hempseed-crusted tofu cutlets over spinach salad, chia seed pudding with 90% cacao, personal finance podcast, Goodwill drop-off, no more wire hangers ever, I can see all the dust in the air, I can see all the dirt on the baseboards, it's irresponsible to the community that I'm not fluent in Spanish, I should read *Moby Dick,* I should call my grandma, what if I never run a sub-two-hour half marathon, what if I never publish the Great American Novel, what if I never measure up to these benchmarks of success that I've set only for myself and would never ask of anyone else, guided meditation, bed at 10.

I'll get back to you the second I'm sniff and re-wear the T-shirt, jeans off the floor, just buy more underwear and leave the shopping bag in the corner for a couple of weeks, *The Girls Next Door* marathon, how early in the day does the pizza place deliver, six hours of screen time on this device, Pringles dust, run the Roomba.

Others

You will never be able to convince me that people everywhere in the world are not just people. That's one thing to social media's credit: it makes it much harder for governments or those in power to create convenient enemies through othering.

Because you can sell me the story my whole life that people in the Middle East are fundamentally different from me, and therefore their lives matter less, or that immigrants or refugees, based off of the random circumstances under which we were born, deserve less than I do. But you put a phone into the hand of some funny Gen Z kid saying, "Get ready with me to get bombed!" and it shatters the whole illusion. It's much harder to other us when we see proof of how similar we are.

I'm not saying that everyone everywhere is all the same in every way. Obviously, religion, and politics, and the respective spin of our history books, and the stories we're taught from childhood, are different. But if you look in any country in this world, we are all just human animals experiencing the same range of pain and pleasure.

We have all felt cold ocean waves or trickling river water on the tops of our feet on a hot day, and we have all held onto each other's forearms to steady ourselves because we're losing our balance from laughing so hard, and we have all sat down for a meal with people we love and felt total warmth and comfort.

You can't convince me that I am, in some way, a special, different, other thing from people who are suffering. It's just not going to happen.

Vroom Vroom Grrrr

Some things that have the same energy: the blackened tip of the yellow marker that will never draw a clean sun again. Coming face-to-face with the spot of blue mold when you're halfway through the bite. The sweaty locker room smell in the back of the school bus.

The saliva pooling around your tongue as you accept the inevitability that you're going to throw up today. When your eyes zoom out in the aisle full of seasonal plastic items, and you remember that every Target has one of these, and that all the contents will end up somewhere.

Sending the text, holding your breath, and watching the dot dot dot appear and disappear as they work out how to respond. Feigning nonchalance at the checkout when there's a fair chance the card won't go through. Discovering the word means something different from how you've always used it.

The sticky feeling in your soft palate, the swell in your nostrils, the water along the brims of your eyes that could be allergies, but are probably a cold. When you anxiously track the package, rip it open, and discover that you ordered the wrong thing.

Watching yourself in the dressing room, jumping and shimmying into the jeans whose button won't close. When the test is all the things you didn't study and none of the things you did.

The first snip of the haircut starting way too high up. The vroom vroom grrrr of wheels stuck in mud, illuminated maintenance lights, brushing the snow off the windshield just for an avalanche to fall down from the roof.

Time Travel

I feel like if we could time travel, we mostly wouldn't. If you watch *The Office* ten times a year because you're too tired to pick something else, you're not going to the Renaissance. If you don't go to Hollywood Boulevard or Times Square because it's crowded and smells like pee, you're not going to the Colosseum.

My friend who takes transatlantic flights for concerts, *she* might go see Shakespeare's Globe. My relative who hikes into the depths of Yellowstone without a GPS and builds an igloo, *he* might meet Lewis and Clark. But I didn't go to a wedding because I didn't want to drive to Wisconsin. I really just highly doubt that I'm gonna go travel through time.

You know there'd be a couple people who would be so annoying about it, like, "Just save up your credit card points! You can go see Jesus's sermon on the mount! It's sponsored by Wells Fargo," and somebody who would be like, "Come with us to my grandparents' wedding! It's gonna be so beautiful. It's in Jim Crow Mississippi."

I could fly to Asia and I haven't. I could learn German and I haven't. I haven't seen *Anora* yet because I'm too tired to watch a movie after 9 PM.

Time travel?

Ankle Weights

Sometimes life feels like take medicine, take vitamins, choke down coffee, drag bristles across teeth, put all your strength into putting on clothes. Sometimes it feels like translate from one language to another, physical exertion to participate in conversation, complicated math to take bites of food, walk a quarter mile behind the runners wearing ankle weights and a parka, stare blankly at the rushing cars, try to conjure dream memories of joy.

But then again, if you can remember, if you can receive that message from the other side, it would say that life has also felt like finding someone so funny that you want to write down everything they say so you can keep it, and rewinding that one part of the song because it makes your whole body hum, and lighting a teakwood candle with an extra-long match for the ambiance, and bouncing ideas off someone who makes you feel like a deep well of creativity, and arranging a veggie tray to eat in a crowded kitchen, and a healing steam shower, and feeling comforted by your own quiet company.

And, of course, it's felt like driving through winding mountain roads, where everything is big and green and gold, and taking a long, deep breath, and thinking, *Are you seeing this? Are you seeing this right now?*

Scrolling

Here's a conspiracy theory, here's horrible news, here's a city that's better than the one you live in, here's the worst city on Earth— why aren't you grateful? Here's a cute dress, here's the factory where children make it, here's how to save money, here's how to abolish money, here's something that will finally make you beautiful if you buy it, here's where people are suffering, here's how to do self-care, here's how much plastic you're eating, here's how many animals are suffering from the things you're buying, here's someone living their life to the fullest while you scroll, here's someone making bank by making things that you can scroll to, here's how many things you could accomplish if you just got up already, here's a reminder to reduce stress, here's a recipe for manifesting your dream life, here's the secret to positive thinking, here's a prison camp, here's how worldly possessions are making you evil, here's how booking that service will make your skin ten years younger, here's how the desire to look younger is ruining your life and making you look older, here's how your attention is creating an unstoppable AI that will lead to your doom, here's how not paying attention is a privilege, here's how you can reduce the pain in the world by watching videos of it, here's how you need to log off and touch grass, here's how grass is ruining the ecosystem, here's how many people are lonely, and here's how it's your fault.

Bubbles

We don't appreciate bubbles. These perfect, iridescent, spherical orbs that float on air, and reflect light, and pop on your fingertip? That you can will into existence with your breath like a god? The universe created these and was like, "You guys gotta check this out!" and we were like, "That's amazing!" and then after age six, we were like, "What else you got?"

So it was like, "Okay, what if on summer evenings, these little bugs lit up like stars and they pulsed in the air and you could hold them in your hand?" And we were like, "Yeah, that's okay. What else you got?"

So it was like, "Okay, what if over the coldest, darkest corners of Earth, sometimes the sky was highlighter pink and shocking aquamarine and vibrant teal and smeary magenta?" And we were like, "Yeah, that's pretty cool, but it's kind of hard for me to see it."

So the universe was like, "Okay, what if I make the sun the exact right distance away, the moon the exact right size, so that occasionally the moon covers the sun, turns it into nighttime for a couple minutes during the day, and you can watch it from your own yard?" And we were like, "Yeah, that's pretty cool, but it doesn't happen very often."

So then the universe was like, "What if on every coastline, everywhere in the world, ocean waves crashed and foamed all day long, creating perfect, iridescent, spherical orbs that float on air, and reflect light, that you can pop on your fingertip?" And we were like, "Eh."

Reasons I'm Glad To Be Alive In This Century

An elderly person can tell me about a TV show they vaguely remember from their childhood, and without even knowing its name, I can tap on a piece of glass and conjure it for them out of thin air.

I can raise an airplane window shade and come face-to-face with golden hour cumulus clouds.

I can wonder when horses were first domesticated, or who founded the oldest still-printing wallpaper company, and I can know the answer within five seconds.

I can pull up to a drive-thru and casually grab some lifesaving antibiotics.

I can go to a craft store, buy a heap of supplies, watch a YouTube tutorial, and handmake a quilt for a baby I can't wait to meet.

I can remember the birthday of a little girl I rode rollerblades with in 1998, and I can send a vibration, and a flash of light, and words of love directly to her pocket.

I can look over from the passenger seat and admire the curve of his nose and the wrinkles by his eyes and I can catch the moment his lip hitches to form the smile that still knocks me the hell out.

I Do Not Want To Camp

I do not want to camp. I do not want to glamp. I do not want to sleep on a futon, on a cot, or zipped inside a polyester bag. I will lie on the grass under the stars, but only if you can guarantee minimal mosquitos, and only if, when we're done, I don't have to brush my teeth by pouring bottled water onto the bristles outside.

I do not want to use an outhouse. I do not want to squat in the woods. I do not want someone to say, "There's no soap, but there's hand sanitizer."

I do not want to eat food that's been sitting in a box out in the sun. I do not want to eat food wrapped in cling wrap, or microwaved in plastic, or that's been in a cooler so long that it's now damp from melting ice.

When I was twenty and you asked me, "How many of your friends can share this hotel room with two queen beds?" my answer was, "I don't know, nine? Twelve?" My answer now is between one and two. One and two. If there's a third person, I'll act like I'm totally fine with it, but I won't be totally fine with it.

I'm not saying I wouldn't endure these circumstances. I'm saying that I don't want to spend money to seek them out. I do not want my vacation to consider bears because I don't want to be where bears don't want me to be. I don't want to be where soap isn't.

Heaven's Pink

If we meet up in heaven in a hundred years, let's do a night of our twenties together again. Let's jump and thrash under fuchsia lights until our sweat shimmers like sequins. Let's smudge eyeliner and glitter in a bar bathroom mirror with a backdrop of Sharpied jokes and philosophical quotes.

Let's pour the sparkliest bottle of Barefoot Moscato into coffee cups for an upward elevator toast. Let's scream and smoke our throats hoarse and let's fountain gulps of pool water out of fish lips. Let's debate the best Beatle on a bean bag chair, let's try to peel a grapefruit between our two mouths with no hands allowed.

Let's sardine a crowd into a hotel room, start some shit on Twitter, chug the water at the bottom of the ice bucket. Let's three-legged race across downtown and find pharmacy foam flip-flops to replace your broken heel. Let's fall on the bed with sparking livewire bodies and kick the quilt into a heap because if anything touches us we'll burn this Marriott down.

Let's eat the breakfast spaghetti cold and turn the place inside out searching for your passport. Let's get some half-sleep with cheeks pressed against bus windows that smell of exhaust and laugh at our blackened feet and call spearmint gum temporary toothpaste.

Let's run across the 101 and float up Sunset as the sun turns on and steal a cross-body bag full of rose-colored smog.

It Is That You Are

I'm afraid of what AI will do to the entertainment industry, I am. But I'm not afraid of losing my drive to consume art made by messy, judgmental, beautiful, empathetic, cruel, and kind human minds. I will be making art and I will be seeking it out. AI can reiterate things people have said, simulate the way people feel, but it can't tell me your story of being alive.

I will always want to know what religion did to you, and what memory of your grandmother breaks your heart, and what mortifying teenage blunder keeps you up at night, and what food from your culture transports you to another country with the first bite, and how your heart swells when you experience live music in a crowd of people buzzing in unison, and if you've ever laid in the shadows of your bedroom curtains and lightly raked your fingernails up and down the back of someone who trusts you with their secrets.

AI can tell me "people die," but it cannot make me sit with you in *your* grief. AI can tell me "people give birth," but it cannot tell me what you saw behind *your* eyelids while bleeding on a table to bring a soul into the world.

It can tell me "people fall in love," but it cannot rub a calloused thumb along the veins in my arm and calm the anxiety in my heart, because the point of you is not how you act. It's that you are you. It is that you are.

Part 5

Falling In

"I'm never late to the party
if I'm late to the party with you."

—Kacey Musgraves, "Late to the Party"

What Do Women Want?

What do women want? Women want to wear natural fibers that breathe, in colors that flatter their skin tone, that are structured enough to be shapely, but loose enough to not be restrictive. They want to drink a little drink that's sweet, but not overwhelmingly so, and have a little dessert bite with depth.

And they want to be stretched out on a sun-warmed lounge chair, next to a gently swaying body of water, and they want to be under the shade of a wide-brimmed hat, reading a novel whose spine is flexible enough to bend over on itself, that's mostly witty and emotional conversations, but you feel changed by the end of it.

They want to doze off in that in-between space, where you can still perceive the murmur of people around you, and the seagulls cawing, and the smell of the salt in the air, but your eyes are heavy, and you're watching the colorful sun spots behind them, and when you fade back to the surface, you feel rested and peaceful, and you're surprised to feel the touch of a hot person's hand on your thigh saying, *We have dinner reservations.*

And they want that person, while they're getting ready, to ask them questions about the book they're reading, and listen curiously, because it's an honor to hear their perspective on something.

And they want the sun to have kissed their cheeks, so they still feel warm when they come out of the shower, but now they want the sun to be low in the sky, as they sit seaside and are offered a stoneware plate piled with an expert balance of nourishment to flavor, and they want to gaze out at the blue gradient of the sky meeting the water, and they want the person across the table from them to be gazing at them with the same reverence.

More or less.

It's Entirely Possible

You know, it's entirely possible that one day you're going to wake up next to someone who you want to talk to before you've even opened your eyes, who you want to make out with before either of you has even brushed your teeth, whose chest is going to feel like it was carved specifically to fit your cheek.

And it's entirely possible that the way their messy hair and white t-shirt are going to seem to glow in the early morning kitchen light is going to make you feel like you could melt into a puddle and slip out the back door, but you can't right now, because they're making you breakfast.

And they're putting fresh lime and avocado and salsa in a breakfast burrito, and they're grilling it on both sides, because they know you like it that way, and they're wrapping it in foil, even though it's a little bit of a waste, because they know that's the way you like to eat it. And you're going to grind their coffee before you make yours, because they like theirs a little coarser than you like yours.

And you're going to sit together, and you're going to talk about what your friends are posting on social media, and you're going to talk about the movie you watched last night, and the movie you watched ten years ago, and you're going to talk about the news, and you're going to ask each other's opinions, and you're going to realize that you could do this every single day for the rest of your lives.

And it might not happen. But it is entirely possible that it will. It's entirely possible that some person is going to feel more home to you than home does.

Pride And Prejudice

Hear me out. I get a brown paper bag full of fresh bagels and some almond cream cheese. I find a box of old magazines on a Buy Nothing group. I bring them over.

You put on a Meg Ryan movie, you make coffee, you put out slices of oranges and strawberries. We spend the morning flipping through the magazines and flopping around on the couch.

We're making jokes about all the old clothes and all the old celebrities, and then we find a bunch of craft supplies and make vision boards. It's 50% a joke, like "I wish I were in the Maldives with Owen Wilson," and it's 50% really earnest, like "Oh my gosh, that thing that you say you want to be, you already are! Everyone always says that about you."

And then you'll be like, "That's so funny that you would say that, because I was just bragging about *you* the other day," and then we'll say, "There's a lot of green on these posters for two people who've been inside for so long." We'll go for a walk.

The day is beautiful, blue sky, fluffy white clouds. There's tons of people outside to watch. There's like an old guy doing tricks on a skateboard who probably doesn't need that much attention, there's like a crowd of little kids being wild with sidewalk chalk.

And then I'll be like, "Oh my gosh, my feet are so muddy, what am I, Elizabeth Bennet?" And you'll be like, "Ninety-five or oh five?" And I'll be like, "Great point, should we go watch both?" and you'll be like, "We need to watch both."

Order takeout, watch *Pride and Prejudice* for like seven hours, debate the merits of wet shirts versus hand flexes. Darcy what I mean?

Sweat And Glitter

I don't think I was put on this planet to work a job. I think I was born to fry Roma tomatoes in oil and garlic and pile them on top of spaghetti with shreds of basil plucked right off the plant.

And to drive around with one hand out the window and feel a rush of summer air filling my palm and then trickling through my fingers, and to spin around on a dance floor making my funny friends laugh until we end the night with our hair full of sweat and glitter, and to chase the chocolate around the circumference of a soft serve twist cone, and to still have my childhood best friends' phone numbers memorized, and to make eye contact with someone from across the room, knowing it'll make them blush, and then watching it happen.

And to not be able to watch the curtain call of any musical without tearing up, and to hear a song for the first time and think, *well, that's that, I'm going to love this song for the rest of my life,* and to dip my pinky in the frosting and decide that it needs more lemon.

And to warm the backs of my thighs on poolside concrete while I sip on a drink with a tiny umbrella in it, and to smell every candle in the store, and to hike to the top of the hill, look around, and then feel the roller coaster leap in my chest as I run down the other side, and to read a line in a book and think, *I thought I was the only one who felt that way.*

Asymmetrical Ceramics

To give you a rough outline, I just want something along the lines of a gauzy muslin canary yellow sundress, perfectly worn-in sneakers, canvas tote bag, over-ear headphones playing Carole King's *Tapestry*, a glass jar with black iced tea and those smooth, cylindrical ice cubes with hollow centers, and the juice from a lemon wedge, and the lemon wedge still bobbing around inside.

And I want to drink that on a sidewalk that takes me past friends sunbathing on a porch, and a really busy restaurant patio with yellow umbrella tables and bottomless mimosas, and someone playing a trumpet at a little art fair, where kids are running around and laughing, and someone's selling funky earrings and asymmetrical ceramics and paintings of my city skyline and polished rose quartz.

And I want the sidewalk to take me to an antique shop, where I want to scavenge through shelves full of chaos, and I want Ella Fitzgerald in my headphones while I dig through a shoebox of sepia-toned photos of strangers in love.

And then I want the sidewalk to take me to a used bookstore, where I want to pet an old orange tabby cat who's extra soft from resting in a patch of sun by the front window, and I want to run my finger along the bumps of spines of books old and new, and I want to find something so specific to a person I love, that after the cashier slips it in my tote bag, I want to picture their sunny smile for my entire walk back home to them.

Daydreams

Here are some free things you can daydream about today.

It's your first morning on the newly colonized moon, and you're skipping through zero gravity dust to the greenhouse full of fresh produce, where you can float quietly and write a letter back home while you watch the earthrise.

Or you're a square of dark chocolate, melting into a steamy cup of milk, under an espresso machine waterfall. You wear a fluffy dollop of whipped cream like a crown.

Or you're at an all-expenses-paid, weeklong wellness spa retreat, and your only job there is to do the kind of exercise you like to do, and get skin treatments and massages, and do meditations. And the only decision you have to make the entire time is what you want to eat from the highly curated menu, designed specifically for your desires and needs.

Or you're 85 years old, reading an article about your storied career and your contributions to your field. You're looking through the comments, finding some from people who love you, and some from people you've never met, but who respect your work from afar.

Or you're a bath bomb, fizzing and flowery and glittery, swaying and spinning and dissipating in the water.

Or you're in love. Just the regular, human kind, here on Earth.

Sizzling Skillet

Mid-summer, mid-afternoon, we're seeing an A24 movie in the back row center of a theater with reclining seats and blasting air conditioning. We're there before the trailers start, we're wearing leggings and fuzzy boots inappropriate for the outside weather. The enormous tub of popcorn is in your lap, and I'm covertly unwrapping contraband dark chocolate peanut butter cups inside my sweatshirt pocket and passing them to you like love notes. We forget who we are for two hours.

We come out, blinking and disoriented that the sun is still up, with lots to discuss from the movie, so we move the operation to a Mexican restaurant. It has cinder block walls, tile tabletops, crepe paper decorations. The vinyl booths have cracks in them. The basket of chips is still hot, and some of them are glistening with oil. The salsa is flowing. We're drinking from fish bowls with lime and cayenne on the rims. Selena Gomez is singing "I love you like a love song, baby" over the speaker and we're dancing in our seats.

My sizzling skillet of veggie fajitas causes a scene, and we almost do, too, because the music's bringing back old memories, and we're laughing until our cheeks burn. So we leave a big tip, and we leave with big takeout boxes, because we're so over-full on sugar and salt and love for each other.

The Tomatoes

I used to date people who made me say things like, "I know you call me a bitch as a term of endearment, but do you think you could try saying something nice to me sometime, just to see how it goes?"

I am married to a man who says to me, "I did not know tomatoes could taste good until you cut the tomatoes."

Hillside Home

She probably doesn't want a mansion. She probably wants a little hillside home with a kitchen with copper heirloom pots hanging on the rack, and cascading houseplants and mismatched ceramic mugs on open shelving, and abundant fresh food in her retro green fridge, and a moka pot on her restored highback gas stove.

And a projector for playing old movies, and a knit blanket draped over the arm of an elegant, curved sofa, and a bookshelf full of treasures and trinkets to remind her of places she's been and people she's loved.

And a spiral staircase leading up to a hallway collaged with framed photos and handwritten love letters and theatre tickets and cross-stitch art.

And a comfy bed, pushed against the window facing the ocean, in a tight but airy room, with a vaulted ceiling, and exposed rafters, and a skylight that lets the moon glow down on her antique vanity and its glass perfume bottles and hooks displaying both dainty finery and costume jewelry.

And she wants a soaking tub on a checkerboard black and white tile floor, underneath a bespoke chandelier, next to a glass-front cabinet full of fluffy towels, behind which there's a secret safe containing five million dollars and the keypad that controls the surrounding bulletproof fallout dome that's impervious to the effects of climate disasters and invisible to anyone uninvited.

The Field Across The Street From The Church

I don't know how often you're in the area, but if you ever find yourself in the Midwest suburbs in June of 2007, I just got my driver's license, and I have big plans for the summer, so hit me up.

First, I'm gonna scrunch my hair to a crisp. I'm gonna eat a Kudos bar while I watch the two hours of *Dawson's Creek* that play on TBS in the morning, and then I'm gonna put on a deep v-neck tunic with a lace tank top underneath, a denim skirt, Old Navy flip flops, a decorative belt, and an enamel necklace. I'm gonna head over.

I'm gonna pop in the mix CD I burned for the occasion— it's metallic pink and it says "Summer in the Mazda" on it in Sharpie— and it has fifteen illegally downloaded tracks, beginning with Christina Aguilera's cover of "Car Wash" from the *Shark Tales* soundtrack, and then ranging from "Buy U A Drank" to "Hey There Delilah." We're gonna pull into the gas station parking lot, we're gonna leave the windows down while we crank "Fergalicious," so everyone knows we're hot while we dig through the cupholders for enough spare change to buy a quarter tank of gas and two enormous styrofoam cups full of fountain Coke.

We're gonna take those to the field across the street from the church, we're gonna pick and peel blades of grass, we're gonna play that game we invented where we flick a piece of mulch in the air and turn into gods who can make anything happen, like that guy who's mean to you stubs his toe, that teacher we hate gets the *Hannah Montana* theme song stuck in her head, our friendship never changes even after we graduate and move to different cities next year.

And then we're gonna play on the swing set, and we won't be sure if we're two adults pretending to be kids, or two kids pretending to be adults, but we will know, as we watch our bare feet against the big blue sky, and we synchronize our movements, and we talk about our hopes, and our fears, and our insecurities, that no two people have ever been as made-for-each-other as we are in this moment.

Picnic Basket

If she's ever said she wants you to be more romantic, here's what you're going to do. The next time she orders coffee in front of you, you're going to write down her order in your Notes app. You're going to tell her one day that you have a date planned around lunchtime. You're not going to tell her what it is.

You're going to show up with that coffee, with her name written on it in Sharpie, and a little heart next to it. (If you're a man, it's especially cute to see a hand-drawn heart in a man's handwriting, but you don't have to be a man for this to work.)

You're going to take her to a bookstore and say, "Pick out two things: one, something you would like to read today, and two, something you think I would like to read today." You're going to take these to a park. You're going to pull out—surprise!— a picnic blanket and a picnic basket. (This works best if you have a car. Sorry, I'm American.)

What's inside the basket? Oh, it's her favorite takeout that you ordered on your phone last time, so you already have her order! It's Chinese food, or those little sandwiches you know she likes.

You're going to sit there, you're going to eat together, you're going to read together. At some point, you're going to take a little selfie of the two of you together. (This is important.)

You're going to enjoy your afternoon, and after that, you're going to print out that selfie as a 4x6 photo. You're going to slip it into that book as a bookmark. She's going to find it.

Oh my gosh, she's going to tell all her friends how cute you are.

Beach Day

Here's the itinerary. Little shower, big iced coffee, cook breakfast, beach day.

Beach swim, beach walk, beach flop around on a towel. Beach carton of strawberries and we're all making a pile in the middle of the tops. Beach crusty bread, creamy sauce sandwich, beach cold drink with a little bit of condensation on the can. Beach bury each other's feet in the sand, beach look for a seashell in every color and line them up to make a rainbow.

Little shower, couch reset. Phone charge, reality show.

Pool swim. Pool bob around laughing and splashing each other like little kids, pool lean against the wall and close your eyes and pretend to be a lizard sunning itself on a rock. Big towel, cover up, ice cream cone. Shop that only sells keychains and sand dollars. Shop that only sells monkeys carved out of coconuts.

Big shower, cute outfit, hang around the kitchen, greasy chips out the bag, ice in the blender, squeezing limes.

Beachfront outdoor restaurant, get a couple entrees and put them in the middle of the table so everyone can have a little bite of everything.

Bonfire. Roasting sticks, write each other's names in the air with smoke. Fall asleep on top of the sheets, under the ceiling fan. Repeat.

The Most Intimate Of Intimacies

The most intimate of intimacies is stepping back to see the paint samples from their point of view. It's ladling their salsa bar favorites into little condiment cups. It's a mental rolodex of movie quotes, applied in contexts that only make sense to the two of you. It's *it would be easier to do it alone, but I'd rather do it together.*

The most intimate of intimacies is picking each other's Cards Against Humanity. It's wordlessly conducting an entire conversation from opposite sides of the party. It's a one-handed neck massage in the car. It's *it's fun to go out, but it's better to come in.*

The most intimate of intimacies is knowing their sports team's coach's name (Shane something). It's giving them the bigger pieces of broccoli in the prettier bowl. It's them insisting they like the picture you picked, and you insisting you like the way they hung it. It's seeing their eye color in the lake.

The most intimate of intimacies is *tell me more about it*. It's *I knew you could do it*. It's *you constantly amaze me*. It's *I have you memorized, and yet there's so much more to know*.

Mornings You Might Wake Up In

You might wake up in a cold sweat, replaying dream visions of mushroom clouds and bioweapons, mass shooters and their memes, artificial intelligence in the hands of the artificially empathetic.

You might wake up in a gray fog, all the highs and lows compressed, monotony with no contrast, no borders, no dynamics.

You might wake up on a glittering Christmas, all tiny running feet, and ripping shiny paper, and Nat King Cole, and terrycloth robes, and chocolate before breakfast.

You might wake up in a pool of blood, cursed with feminine pain tolerance, and anger suppression, and burden carrying, and artful starvation.

You might wake up in the crook of their knees, the front of your heart against the back of theirs, a pulsing circuit of beats and breaths and warmth.

You might wake up in the pain that sleep can't erase, with the head throb, the stomach pit, the drained eyes, the dry mouth, the spine shiver.

You might wake up in the sleepless days that blend together endlessly, no top and no bottom, no beginning and no end, just blurry eyes and heavy feet and uninterrupted weariness.

You might hear the song, read the line, watch the film, see the painting, smell the herb, feel the water, hug the child, run the path, stick the landing, make them laugh, make them feel, make them safe, find the person, kiss the neck, take the breath, and wake up inside.

Quiet Forest

What if you wake up in a patch of sun, with the walls glowing yellow, dappled with the flickering, leafy shadows from the woodland trees outside a shining, fog-glazed window?

And you sink your toes into the high-pile carpet, and stretch your arms high above your head, and skip to the kitchen, and pile into a pan potatoes and peppers and onions and spinach and chickpeas, as steam swirls from the spout of the whistling tea kettle?

And you artfully arrange two plates with fanned slices of Cara Cara oranges, and pour the contents of the pan onto flour tortillas, and drizzle them with hot sauce, as warm arms hug you from behind, and help you carry everything to the little textured glass table on the balcony?

And you look out over miles of quiet forest, and you point out a doe and her fawn resting in golden grass, and you rest your head on the shoulder next to you, and they refill your mug and help you pick today's hike?

And you spend hours on dirt paths, smelling pine needles, collecting marbled orange and yellow leaves, listening to the wind in the trees, and the birds, and a soothing voice telling you their thoughts and venerating yours?

And you spend the late afternoon inside, snacking and reading and napping, and gently dropping Billie Holiday records onto the turntable?

And you spend after dark with hot tub jets massaging your shoulders, and a comfortable silence with the person you love, and the tall, dark shadows of trees against a backdrop of thousands of stars? What if?

Muscle Memory

Some things that have the same energy: the smell of vanilla extract while you cream together butter and brown sugar with a wire whisk, the way your breathing slows as the credits start to roll after a good movie, unfolding a piece of lined notebook paper to find a letter from an old friend that's fabric-soft from age, rubbing your feet together like a cricket under the covers on a cold night, the way the bright lights over the baseball stadium turn the night sky an otherworldly warm dark blue, the way your sleeping child body instinctively knew you'd pulled onto your street at the end of a long drive, melting ice cream atop syrupy skillet-fried peaches, worn pajama pants with a waistband that sits perfectly atop your hips, muscle memory finding the notes on an instrument you haven't played in years, the way the music from inside the bar sounds while you wait for a car on the curb, the smell of a rubbery yellow inner tube in a chlorinated pool, a grandparent's loopy cursive on a birthday card envelope, knowing someone's face well enough that you would notice if a single freckle were out of place, reading the final sentence of a book… as slowly as you can… and holding it to your chest… as you turn the last page.

Mornings You Might Wake Up In

Thank You

Thank you to John, Jess, PJ, and Heather for being early readers/encouragers, to Carina for her copyediting ("gentle-domming" probably does need a hyphen), and to Jordan for his design work.

Thank you to TikTok, 78 degrees, pickled red onion and habanero, modal interchanges, Nicaragua Segovia dark roast espresso, runner's highs, internal rhyme, alliteration, Wellbutrin, Wikipedia, Wednesdays at 2PM, mustard yellow, lilac, coral, olive green, chartreuse, public libraries, orange calcite, Topanga Canyon, the rust belt, Hilton Head, Goodbye South, Vietti Barbera d'Asti Trevigne, Impossible Nuggets, hydrangeas, peonies, Kentucky bluegrass, the law of attraction, cancer research, everyone who watched the videos, everyone who encouraged me while not knowing how to watch the videos, everyone who leaves me buzzing and poetic, everyone who taught me to never get bored of the moon, everyone who loves me for who I am despite who I am occasionally.

Thank you to the gray-blue eyes, the reason I'm alive.

About The Author

Hayley G. Hoover writes poems that sound like social media posts and social media posts that sound like poems. She lives in a century-old home full of century-old books.

Find her online at @hayleyghoover

"Do you ever just talk normally and not like an overwritten 'witty' young adult novel from a girl's perspective where the whole thing is just her inner thoughts?"

—TikTok comment from an X-Men fan account

www.ingramcontent.com/pod-product-compliance
Lightning Source LLC
Chambersburg PA
CBHW052142070526
44585CB00017B/1932